CW01512642

Original title:
Tawny Leaves Across the Elf Slat

Copyright © 2025 Swan Charm
All rights reserved.

Author: Swan Charm
ISBN HARDBACK: 978-1-80562-040-2
ISBN PAPERBACK: 978-1-80563-561-1

Flickers of Light in the Dusky Hollow

In the hollow where shadows play,
Flickers of light dance and sway.
Glowing orbs in the midnight air,
Whispering secrets with gentle flair.

Mossy stones and ancient trees,
Breath of the night carried on the breeze.
Each twinkle tells a tale of old,
Of courage, heart, and dreams untold.

Flickering lanterns, fears dispel,
In dusky corners where magic dwells.
Echoes of laughter, soft and bright,
Guide lost souls through the endless night.

A glint, a shimmer, a breathless pause,
Nature's wonder without a cause.
In this realm where dreams take flight,
The dusky hollow thrives on light.

So linger here, dear traveler bold,
In the stories that the shadows hold.
Let flickers of hope in your heart ignite,
And follow the glow into the night.

The Ethereal Call of the Quiet Wood

In the quiet wood, where silence sings,
A gentle call from unseen wings.
The rustle of leaves, a melodic tune,
Under the shade of the silvered moon.

Whispers of thickets, soft and low,
Guide the wanderer where secrets flow.
In the depths of green, a promise lies,
Echoed in the breeze that softly sighs.

Amidst the shadows, moments weave,
Magic sways in the hearts that believe.
The ethereal call, a beckoning grace,
Invites all souls to embrace their place.

Branches entwined in a delicate dance,
Filling the night with a potent chance.
To hear the stories of long ago,
In the quiet wood, where wonders grow.

So step with care upon this ground,
For in each corner, joys abound.
With every heartbeat, let spirits lift,
Answer the call, the greatest gift.

Dance of the Woodland Beings

In the twilight glow, the woodland stirs,
A dance unfolds, where silence blurs.
Elfin laughter, twinkling bright,
In harmony with the fading light.

Sprightly feet upon the moss,
Each twirl and leap, a moment glossed.
Fingers weave through the night's embrace,
Crafting a spell of time and space.

Around the brook, a sparkling flight,
Whirling sprites in the soft moonlight.
The trees sway gently to the sound,
Of music born from the earth's own ground.

Each flicker, each sparkle, a story told,
Of love, of loss, and days of old.
With every heartbeat, they twine and spin,
In the woodland's heart, where magic begins.

So join this dance, let spirits soar,
In the symphony of the night's allure.
The woodland beings, ancient and free,
Invite your soul to blend with the tree.

Whispers of Change Beneath the Stars

In the quiet of night, with stars aglow,
Whispers of change begin to flow.
The sky adorned with wishes bright,
Promises woven in silver light.

Each twinkle holds a heartfelt prayer,
For dreams forgotten and burdens bare.
Beneath the stars, the universe sighs,
In the vastness, hope never dies.

The autumn winds brush past with grace,
A tender touch on the world's face.
Leaves surrender, a graceful fall,
Answering nature's sacred call.

In the fabric of night, truths unveil,
With every whisper, a wondrous tale.
Change flickers softly, like fireflies,
Guiding the lost through starlit skies.

So heed the whispers, let them align,
For change is woven in the divine.
Beneath the stars, what was must cease,
Embrace the night, find your peace.

A Lament for the Harvest Moon

The moon hangs low, a golden sphere,
Whispers of harvest, sweet and clear.
Fields of plenty, now lie bare,
Echoes of laughter float in the air.

Yet shadows creep, as night falls fast,
Memories linger, of summer past.
Crisp leaves crunch beneath my feet,
In this twilight, my heart skips a beat.

Once, joy danced in every light,
Binding our souls with every sight.
Now the chill winds sigh with gloom,
A sharp reminder, lost is the bloom.

Oh, harvest moon, your glow so bright,
Illume the mourners on this night.
Guide us gently through the tears,
And bind our hearts through tangled years.

In silver silence, dreams take flight,
As shadows weave through the soft twilight.
We gather round to share our pain,
In the harvest moon's eternal reign.

Shadows that Speak of Change

In the dusky dusk, where whispers play,
The shadows shift, they twist and sway.
Each corner turned, a secret shared,
The pulse of change, in silence bared.

Ancient trees hold tales untold,
Their gnarled limbs both fierce and bold.
As leaves begin to turn and fall,
We heed the shadows' beckoning call.

The winds of fortune take their way,
With every gust, a price to pay.
Yet from this darkness, light shall rise,
A tapestry woven, in disguise.

In quiet moments, hearts align,
Finding solace in the divine.
As shadows dance beneath the moon,
We yield to change, a gentle tune.

So fear not, friend, for time will flow,
These shadows teach us all we know.
Through every dusk that bids farewell,
New dawns await, as stories swell.

Wandering Spirits Amongst the Woods

Beneath the boughs where shadows creep,
Whispers of spirits gently sleep.
They wander through the twilight haze,
In a dance that weaves through misty days.

With every rustle, tales unfold,
Of enchanted woods and dreams of old.
The trees stand tall, guardians wide,
Cradling secrets the night can't hide.

Footfalls light, on paths unknown,
A quest for truth, in whispers grown.
Echoes of laughter, soft and sweet,
Guide the lost on their journey's feet.

Yet beware, for shadows play,
In the heart of night, they twist and sway.
For every spirit that takes to flight,
There lies a choice, to spark the light.

So roam, dear heart, where magic calls,
Through ancient trees and ivy walls.
In the embrace of the twilight breeze,
Wander with spirits, and find your peace.

Amber Shadows and Fairy Dreams

In the dappled glade where fairies gleam,
Amber shadows weave through a dream.
With laughter light and echoes sweet,
They spin their magic, softly fleet.

Mossy carpets beneath my feet,
Guiding me to where magic meets.
Glimmers sparkle in the twilight air,
Whispers beckon, if I dare.

The moon shines bright on dewy leaves,
Encasing secrets, the heart believes.
With every flutter, every sigh,
The night holds tales that will not die.

Among the thickets, starlight clings,
In harmony with the song that sings.
The dance of shadows, a spiraling waltz,
Holds the heart, in twilight's pulse.

So linger long, and breathe it in,
Let fairy dreams begin again.
In amber shadows, take your flight,
Through the enchanted, velvet night.

Memories Beneath the Arching Boughs

Beneath the boughs where shadows play,
Old memories linger, softly sway.
Whispers of laughter, long since past,
Echo through time, forever cast.

Sunlight filters, golden hue,
Painting the ground in vibrant view.
Every rustle, a silent story,
Of fleeting days, and fading glory.

The scent of earth, rich and deep,
Calls back the dreams that we once keep.
In this haven, time stands still,
Magic woven with a gentle will.

Leaves dance lightly on the breeze,
Carrying secrets from ancient trees.
In every rustling, a voice is found,
Binding the past to the present ground.

So linger here, where memories flow,
Under arching boughs, let your heart grow.
For in these woods, you'll surely see,
The timeless bond of you and me.

The Whispered Secrets of Dusk

Beneath the veil of twilight's grace,
The shadows gather, a gentle embrace.
Secrets whispered in the fading light,
Dance on the edge of the coming night.

Stars begin to twinkle and gleam,
Woven in a silken dream.
Time stretches, as the world slows down,
Nature dons her twilight gown.

The air is thick with tales untold,
Of hearts entwined, and spirits bold.
Listen closely, can you hear?
The murmur of dusk, drawing near.

Crickets chirp their nightly song,
A chorus welcoming the night along.
In this hour, magic and mystery flow,
Painting the world in a softer glow.

So take a breath, let worries fade,
In the twilight, dreams are made.
For in the hush, we find our way,
To whispered secrets of the day.

A Canvas of Nature's Palette

In vibrant hues, the world unfolds,
A canvas brushed with dreams untold.
From emerald greens to sapphire skies,
Nature's art captivates our eyes.

Petals flutter like soft-spun gold,
Stories of summer, gentle and bold.
Through forests thick and rivers wide,
The strokes of beauty, our hearts abide.

The mountains rise, majestic and grand,
Whispering tales of a timeless land.
Each sunrise bursts with fiery red,
A palette where dreams and hopes are fed.

Seasons shift, each brush a change,
From snowy white to autumn's range.
In every glance, a masterpiece lives,
Nature gives more than it ever gives.

So wander through this wondrous space,
Embrace the art, the wild embrace.
For in this canvas, we find our role,
A part of nature, body, and soul.

Spellbound in an Era of Decay

In twilight's grip, when shadows fall,
Time whispers secrets, a haunting call.
Among the ruins, dreams entwine,
In an era where memories dine.

Vines creep softly, reclaim the stone,
Nature's lullaby, a gentle tone.
Ghosts of laughter haunt the air,
In this stillness, a dreamer's prayer.

Once grand towers, now kissing the sky,
Stand witness as the years flit by.
Crumbled arches, stories to tell,
Of days when magic cast its spell.

Rain softens the edges of time,
Each droplet, a whisper, a chime.
In decay lies beauty, raw and true,
A canvas where dreams are born anew.

So linger in this quiet space,
Where time and heart find their place.
For in the ruin, hope remains,
Spellbound by love and lingering chains.

Autumn's Glistening Veil

Leaves fall softly from the trees,
A tapestry of gold and bronze.
Whispers of the chilly breeze,
Heralding winter's quiet songs.

Fields adorned in sunset's hue,
Misty mornings greet the day.
Nature's canvas, rich and true,
As dusk brings autumn's sweet ballet.

Harvest moons in fields aglow,
Pumpkin patches sprawled with cheer.
As shadows stretch and sunsets show,
The glistening veil draws near.

Creatures stir in twilight's hold,
Preparing for their winter's rest.
Stripes of amber, red, and gold,
Whisper secrets, shyly blessed.

In the stillness, hearts renew,
As time weaves stories, warm and bright.
Beneath the stars, life feels anew,
In autumn's glistening light.

Beneath the Canopy's Embrace

In the forest, shadows play,
Dancing leaves, a whispered song.
Branches arch in soft array,
Beneath the canopy so strong.

Sunlight filters through like dreams,
Painting paths in dappled gold.
Where the water gently gleams,
And stories of the wood unfold.

Mossy carpets cradle feet,
Nature's breath, a calming balm.
Every sound, a rhythmic beat,
Wrapped in silence, soft and calm.

Creatures rustle, secrets shared,
In this world, so deep and wise.
Each a spirit unprepared,
To reveal their hidden ties.

Underneath the boughs so wide,
Magic lingers in the air.
In every rustle, every slide,
Hope and wonder flourish there.

Chronicles of the Whispering Wood

Listen close, the trees will tell,
Of ages past, of paths untread.
In the quiet, secrets swell,
Written in the branches' spread.

Echoes float on gentle air,
Voices of the woodlands start.
Nature's lore, a tale to share,
Awakens deep within the heart.

Mysterious shadows drift and dance,
Every step a story born.
In the stillness, you might chance,
To find the dreams that night adorn.

Beneath the arching sycamores,
The laughter of the brook runs free.
Songs of crickets, ancient roars,
Chronicles of wild decree.

From dawn till dusk, the tales unfold,
In every breeze, a whisper's grace.
Nature's heart beats strong and bold,
In the woods, our spirits trace.

When Dreams Tide with the Season

As autumn paints the world in gold,
Dreams awaken with the breeze.
Memories of adventures told,
Woven in the rustling leaves.

Stars align to guide the way,
Where hopes and wishes intertwine.
In the twilight, night and day,
Connect beneath the velvet line.

Each breath carries a silent tune,
As shadows stretch and daylight wanes.
Underneath the harvest moon,
The heart remembers love's remains.

In the dance of falling leaves,
Nature whispers, soft and low.
Let go of what the spirit grieves,
For each ending helps us grow.

When dreams tide with the season's flow,
Embrace the magic lurking near.
In every change, let your heart know,
New chapters await, bright and clear.

Reflections in the Amber Light

In the evening glow so warm,
The shadows dance and softly charm.
Leaves whisper secrets, old and wise,
As amber dreams unfold and rise.

Waves of light caress the trees,
Carrying tales upon the breeze.
Moments held like fleeting sighs,
In twilight's grasp, the world complies.

From silver streams to gilded skies,
The heart of night begins to prize.
With every step, the echoes fade,
In amber light, true peace is made.

Beneath the stars, old stories gleam,
Like ember fires, they softly beam.
In the stillness, hope is sown,
In amber light, we find our home.

A Symphony of Sienna Whispers

In fields where autumn paints with flair,
Sienna tones fill up the air.
A symphony of rustling leaves,
Sings softly to the heart that grieves.

Each note, a flicker of the sun,
Awakens dreams of what's to come.
In gentle curls, the songs entwine,
Revealing paths where shadows shine.

The winds carry tales both bold and bright,
Through golden groves, chasing the light.
Beneath the boughs, cheeks kissed by day,
In whispers sweet, lost fears allay.

As twilight cloaks the vibrant hues,
The music fades, yet still ensues.
In silence deep, the heartbeats blend,
A symphony that will not end.

The Last Breath of Summer's Song

When petals fall in softest sighs,
The last breath of summer flies.
Golden rays begin to wane,
A fleeting warmth, bittersweet pain.

Nature hums a lullaby,
As swallows dance across the sky.
Time drifts by like rippling streams,
Entwined in fading, sunlit dreams.

The air grows crisp, the shadows play,
As dusk prepares to swallow day.
Yet in this whisper, holds a chance,
For every end leads to new dance.

So bid farewell, though hearts may ache,
In every close, a path we take.
The last breath sings, a sweet refrain,
For summer's song shall rise again.

Threads of Gold in the Wind

In morning's light, the world unfolds,
With threads of gold like stories told.
The gentle breeze, it weaves and spins,
A tapestry where hope begins.

Upon the hills, the whispers rise,
From daisies dancing 'neath bright skies.
In every flutter, secrets share,
A promise hangs in vibrant air.

The weaving winds in sparkling flight,
Carry dreams like stars alight.
With every gust, a spirit sewn,
In threads of gold, we're not alone.

So let us wander, hearts unbound,
To find the beauty all around.
In every touch of soft, sweet air,
Threads of gold weave love and care.

Whispers of Autumn's Brush

In the hush of morning light,
Leaves descend, a gentle flight.
Crimson kisses, whispers soft,
Nature's quilt, a treasure troft.

Glistening paths, where shadows play,
Golden edges greet the day.
Squirrels scurry, chattering bright,
In a world of sheer delight.

The air is crisp, a fleeting chill,
Underneath a magic thrill.
A canvas painted, bold and grand,
By the artist's unseen hand.

With every rustle, tales unwind,
Echoes of the trees combined.
History whispers, secrets told,
Life anew, though ages old.

Enchanted Canopy of Gold

Golden crowns on ancient trees,
Dancing softly in the breeze.
Sunlight filters through the green,
Painting shadows, calm and serene.

Beneath the arch of vibrant leaves,
Magic breathes as nature weaves.
Whispers linger in the air,
Enchantments found everywhere.

Nestled nests in branches high,
Songs of robins fill the sky.
A tapestry, rich and vast,
Binding future, present, past.

Trail of acorns, scattered wide,
Where woodland creatures often hide.
A world alive with every stride,
Brimming with a joyous tide.

Dance of the Woodland Spirits

In the twilight's amber glow,
Mischief swirls, a gentle flow.
Mossy carpet, soft and deep,
Where the ancient spirits leap.

Flickering lights like fireflies,
Cast a spell beneath the skies.
Whirl around as shadows play,
In the magic of the day.

Each whisper carried on the wind,
Tales of laughter never pinned.
A harmony of heart and soul,
As the forest finds its role.

Glimmers dance on rippling streams,
Echoing the forest's dreams.
Together weaving, spirits twine,
In their playful, mystic line.

Rustling Secrets Beneath Boughs

Beneath the boughs where secrets lie,
Stories drift like whispers sigh.
Old roots cradle dreams of yore,
While branches guard the hidden lore.

The moonlight drapes in silver threads,
Where unseen paths and legends tread.
A rustle here, a shadow there,
Nature weaves its gentle snare.

In every crack, in every sigh,
Echoes of a fleeting sky.
Time drifts softly, secrets swirl,
In the heart of the ancient world.

Night unfurls its velvet cloak,
With every sound, the forest spoke.
Under starlit, watchful eyes,
Rustling secrets never die.

Secrets of the Forest Floor

Whispers from beneath the green,
A tapestry of life unseen.
Mossy beds where shadows creep,
In silence, ancient secrets sleep.

Amidst the roots, the stories dwell,
Touched by whispers, cast a spell.
Elusive creatures dance and play,
Guardians of the night and day.

Fungi bloom with magic's flare,
Colors bright beyond compare.
Each hidden nook, a tale to weave,
In the forest's heart, we believe.

Footprints left on dewy grass,
Mark the paths where spirits pass.
In every leaf, a promise lies,
Of dreams that sparkle 'neath the skies.

So linger long, and seek, explore,
The secrets of the forest floor.
Each secret shared in twilight's grace,
Is a gift of nature's warm embrace.

The Dance of Drifting Petals

In springtime's breath, the petals twirl,
A gentle sway, a fragrant whirl.
With every gust, they take their flight,
A dance of colors, pure delight.

From cherry blooms to roses bright,
They drift like dreams in soft twilight.
Beneath the sun's warm, golden glow,
They paint the air with love's bright flow.

Like whispers shared on dreams of air,
Their beauty graced without a care.
In softest lands where time stands still,
Their fleeting grace, a tender thrill.

Dancing softly with nature's tune,
Beneath the watchful, watchful moon.
They remind us, as they drift apart,
Of life's fleeting and fragile art.

So let them guide your heart today,
In the dance of petals, find your way.
For every drift is a tale to share,
Of moments cherished, light as air.

Shadows Amongst the Ancient Trees

In twilight's grasp, the shadows play,
Amongst the trees where whispers stay.
Each bark a story, old and wise,
Guarding secrets from prying eyes.

Moonlight filters through the leaves,
As nature's heart gently weaves.
The rustling winds, a soft embrace,
Inviting souls to find their place.

Beneath the canopy, legends loom,
Echoing softly in the gloom.
Each branch a dream, each root a road,
A pathway where the heart may goad.

Lost in shadows, magic thrives,
Where every rustle wakes the lives.
Of creatures cloaked in night's embrace,
Dancing through this timeless space.

The ancient trees, so grand and grand,
Hold stories written in the land.
In hushed reverence, come and see,
The shadows dance, wild and free.

Echoes of a Fading Season

As autumn whispers, leaves descend,
A tapestry where colors blend.
With every gust, the echoes call,
Of nature's dance, a sweet farewell.

The sun dips low, a golden hue,
Reminds us of the warmth we knew.
In every shade, the past remains,
A gentle sigh amidst the pains.

Crisp air carries stories old,
Of summers bright, of nights so bold.
Each rustling leaf recalls the days,
When laughter danced in sunlit rays.

Yet as we walk through fading light,
Embrace the change, both brave and bright.
For echoes linger, sweet and strong,
In every heart, they weave a song.

So cherish now the fading scene,
For time will wrap it in its sheen.
In echoes soft, our hearts we'll find,
The beauty left by seasons kind.

Celestial Dreams Under the Fading Sun

As daylight wanes, the stars awake,
Whispers of night in shadows quake.
The moon ascends with silver grace,
In twilight's arms, we'll find our place.

Dreams take flight on wings of night,
Guided by the soft starlight.
In cosmic dance, our spirits soar,
To realms unseen, forevermore.

The world below, a fleeting glance,
In celestial glow, we dare to dance.
With every sigh, our hopes take wing,
In the dreams that evening brings.

So close your eyes, embrace the glow,
Let the night's magic softly flow.
Beneath the hush of starlit skies,
Where every wish a promise lies.

The Transient Beauty of Glimmering Leaves

In autumn's breeze, the leaves do twirl,
A tapestry of gold unfurl.
Each fleeting moment, painted bright,
A dance of fire in fading light.

Whispers of change in the crisp air,
Nature's splendor, exquisite, rare.
With every rustle, secrets kept,
In the heart of woods where shadows slept.

Oh, how they shimmer, how they gleam,
Reflecting twilight's gentle dream.
In the silence, beauty flows,
A fleeting breath, as nature glows.

Yet soon they fall, upon the ground,
Leaving traces of life unbound.
In each descent, a promise made,
Of spring's return when shades will fade.

So pause, dear friend, and take a view,
For in each leaf, the world is new.
A transient moment, bright and brief,
In every flutter, joy and grief.

Treasures Beneath the Whispering Boughs

In the woods where silence reigns,
The whispering boughs hold ancient pains.
A hidden world, where secrets dwell,
In every shadow, a silent spell.

Beneath the leaves, a treasure lies,
In the rustling song of lullabies.
A gentle heart, a fleeting glance,
Invites us in, to join the dance.

With every step upon the ground,
An echo of the past is found.
The roots entwined, a story shared,
Of dreams forgotten, hopes that dared.

In dappled light, we pause and breathe,
As nature whispers, we believe.
Among the boughs, in comfort's hold,
Lie tales of love and treasures old.

So let us wander, hand in hand,
Through this enchanted, timeless land.
For in the heart of each embrace,
We find our home, our sacred space.

A Symphony of Amber and Bronze

In the fields where silence sings,
Amber waves in gentle sway,
Bronze leaves whisper soft goodbyes,
As twilight bathes the end of day.

Rivers shimmer, gold and bright,
Reflecting tales of yesteryear,
Where laughter mingles with the light,
And secret wishes draw near.

Golden breezes carry dreams,
Through the boughs of ancient trees,
Nature's pulse at sunset gleams,
Awakening a heart's unease.

In every corner, echoes dance,
Creating magic in the air,
Inviting souls to take a chance,
With stories waiting to ensnare.

As night descends, in absence found,
The symphony softens its song,
In amber and bronze, we're spellbound,
Belonging here, forever long.

Shadows in the Twilight Grove

Beneath the trees where whispers dwell,
Shadows play in the evening light,
Each corner holding secrets well,
As day bows softly to the night.

The moon peeks through with silver grin,
Casting dreams on leaves so bold,
Awakening where thoughts begin,
In twilight's grasp we dare be old.

A chorus of creatures sings aloud,
Their voices mingling with the breeze,
In this cloaked and shadowed crowd,
Mysteries curl like slumbering bees.

Rich hues of purple, deep and stark,
Painting stories 'neath the sky,
Where every glance ignites a spark,
And wishes float like moths on high.

In the grove where shadows weave,
Merging time with every breath,
We find the magic we believe,
In twilight's arms, we conquer death.

Flickering Flames of Fall

In autumn's glow, the colors blaze,
Flickering flames in a chilly air,
Leaves like embers dance and craze,
As nature drops her vibrant fare.

Pumpkin smiles and cider's scent,
Fragrant whispers swirl around,
In every heart, a warmth is lent,
While laughter rings, a joyful sound.

Crunching paths beneath our feet,
Golden treasures line the way,
Fires crackle, chapters meet,
As fading light bids us to stay.

Time wanders softly, sweetly spun,
With tales of old that linger long,
In the twilight, we've begun,
To weave our own sweet autumn song.

As dusk descends and shadows blend,
We'll gather close, our stories shared,
Through flickering flames, our hearts will mend,
In fall's embrace, forever cared.

Mystical Hues at Dusk

As daylight fades to pastel dreams,
Mystical hues paint skies aglow,
Awash with blends of gold and creams,
Where whispers of the night will flow.

Stars begin their twinkling dance,
In the velvet of the night,
Each flicker offers soft romance,
A spell cast with sparkling light.

Clouds turn soft in shades divine,
Crimson, lavender, hues of rose,
In this twilight, wonders intertwine,
As every shadow gently grows.

In gardens wrapped in evening's veil,
Fragrant petals start to stir,
Magic lingers on the trail,
Of those who walk, and softly purr.

With every breath, a longing sigh,
Mystical shades embrace our hearts,
As dusk unfolds its lullaby,
To sing of love that never parts.

The Enigma of Dusk's Embrace

As shadows stretch across the glade,
Whispers of twilight softly invade.
The colors dance in a fleeting bloom,
Embracing the night with a hushed loom.

Crickets serenade the coming night,
Stars awaken, a gentle sight.
In the air hangs a bittersweet song,
Where memories linger, deep and strong.

The moon climbs high on a silken thread,
Casting its glow where the wild things tread.
Each secret hidden in the dance of light,
Calls to the heart as it takes flight.

A magic stirs in the cooling air,
An echoing laugh, a whispered prayer.
In dusk's embrace, the world feels whole,
A tapestry woven, an ageless scroll.

Sorrowful Echoes in the Gathering Gloom

As day's embrace begins to fade,
The shadows lengthen, the colors jade.
Echoes of laughter, now shrouded deep,
Lost in the silence where secrets sleep.

Beneath the boughs, the memories weep,
In silence profound, their vigil they keep.
Each whisper of wind tells tales untold,
Of youth and dreams that slipped like gold.

The gathering gloom wraps tight like a shroud,
In the heart of the lost, screams soft and loud.
Where flowers wilt, and shadows combine,
Sorrowful echoes in every line.

Yet through the darkness, a flicker remains,
A pulse of hope beneath aching veins.
In sorrow's embrace, strength can be found,
In the echoes of darkness, love will abound.

The Flickering Flame of the Forgotten Glen

In the heart of the wood where the shadows blend,
Lies a glen forgotten, a long-lost friend.
Where fireflies gather in shimmering flights,
And dreams weave softly in the still nights.

The flickering flame, a guide through the dark,
Illuminates paths with its tender spark.
Amidst the silence, stories unfold,
Of wandering souls and whispers bold.

Amidst the weeds, the flowers grow free,
Claiming the light as their rightful lease.
Each step a promise, each breath a chance,
To wander anew in this curious dance.

The glen holds secrets, both old and wise,
Patched together beneath vast skies.
With every flicker, a tale may be spun,
In the embrace of twilight, life is begun.

A Path Woven with Nature's Echo

Beneath the canopy where wonders reside,
A path unfurls, nature's gentle guide.
Through whispers of leaves and rustling grass,
Each step a journey, moments that pass.

The fragrance of earth fills the hushed air,
Awakening spirits, both wild and rare.
With every footfall on hallowed ground,
Nature's echoes in harmony found.

In the dance of the branches, lost souls can find,
A solace entwined with the open sky.
The heart finds peace in the softest sigh,
As birds weave stories that flutter and fly.

To walk this path is to feel so alive,
Amongst the lush whispers where dreams arrive.
In nature's embrace, let your spirit flow,
For life's greatest treasures are meant to grow.

Whispers of Autumn's Embrace

Leaves flutter down like whispers soft,
In hues of gold that dance aloft.
The air is crisp, a gentle sigh,
As autumn weaves its lullaby.

Beneath the trees where shadows play,
Secrets linger at the close of day.
A tapestry of rust and flame,
Nature speaks, but never names.

Misty mornings, a fleeting glance,
Each breath a spell, a soft romance.
The world adorned in bountiful cheer,
As time unravels, drawing near.

With every step, the crunch of fate,
Every pathway leads to wait.
For in this moment, hearts entwine,
In autumn's grasp, we breathe divine.

When twilight's glow begins to dance,
We find ourselves in nature's trance.
Embraced by whispers, we relent,
In autumn's arms, our hearts content.

Gilded Fragments in the Forest

In woods adorned with gilded grace,
Each step uncovers nature's space.
Fragments of light in dappled form,
Guiding wanderers through the warm.

Beneath the boughs, where fairies dwell,
The air is thick with magic's spell.
Mushrooms peep from mossy beds,
While echoes of the past are shed.

A brook babbles secrets untold,
Carries whispers of the bold.
Time itself seems to hold its breath,
In corners where the wild things rest.

Sunlight filters through the trees,
A symphony upon the breeze.
Each moment dancing in its place,
A fleeting glimpse of nature's grace.

When night descends, the stars take flight,
The forest glows with silver light.
In dreams, we wander, hearts afire,
Among gilded fragments, we aspire.

Enchanted Canopy of Memory

Underneath the silver sky,
Whispers of the past float by.
Leaves above, like thoughts, unwind,
An enchanted canopy intertwined.

Time meanders through the trees,
Carrying echoes on the breeze.
Each rustling leaf, a hidden rhyme,
A brush with moments lost in time.

Mossy paths that lead us home,
In twilight's glow, we are not alone.
Softly murmured secrets fall,
Dance like shadows at night's call.

In this haven, dreams take flight,
Cradled softly by the night.
With every heartbeat, memories bloom,
In the enchanted forest's room.

As we wander, hearts so free,
In this realm of memory.
We weave the threads of what has been,
In the canopy, where time is seen.

Golden Hues in the Twilight

As daylight fades to dusky gold,
In twilight's arms, our stories unfold.
The horizon wraps the world in flame,
Each shadow whispers a lover's name.

The air hangs thick with dreams untold,
While stars awaken, bright and bold.
Fields of amber sway and sway,
Inviting all to dance and play.

Silhouettes of trees embrace the night,
With hints of magic, soft and light.
Paths of wonder, we stroll along,
Underneath an evening song.

As sunset paints with breathless grace,
The heart swells in its warm embrace.
Moments stretch, like time itself,
In the twilight's arms with dreams to delve.

For every sunset holds a new start,
In golden hues, we share our heart.
In this twilight glow, we find our way,
To cherish each fading, perfect day.

Enigmatic Lights in Amber Depths

In twilight's clutch, where shadows creep,
Amber glimmers stir from sleep.
Luminous orbs in gentle sway,
Guide lost hearts along their way.

Whispers of secrets, softly twined,
In the deep, dark woods confined.
Each flicker tells of tales untold,
Of magic woven in threads of gold.

Branches bow with age and grace,
Crimson echoes leave their trace.
Among the leaves, the night draws near,
While distant stars blink, bright and clear.

A dance of phantoms in the gloom,
Illuminate the forest's room.
In every corner, light entwines,
With shadows deep, a fate aligns.

So follow the glow, tread soft and light,
Through mystic fog, into the night.
For those who seek in amber depths,
Shall find within, their heart's true quest.

Songs of the Woodland Creatures

In emerald halls where whispers roam,
The creatures sing, make the woods their home.
Each melody weaves through leaf and bough,
A tapestry of sound, here and now.

With rustling paws and fluttering wings,
The gentle breeze its secret brings.
Hares and foxes dance in the glade,
To the rhythm of dusk as daylight fades.

Owls hoot wisdom from hefty trees,
While nightingales serenade the breeze.
Amidst the ferns, the echoes soar,
Each note a token of ancient lore.

The brook joins in, a bubbly tune,
Under the watchful eye of the moon.
And as the stars dip low to hear,
The woodland's heart becomes clear.

So wander wide, let your spirit roam,
In songs of the wild, you'll find your home.
For in this choir, all lives entwine,
A symphony of nature, simply divine.

Nightfall's Whisper in the Canopy

In dusk's embrace, the trees stand tall,
Casting shadows that gently fall.
Night's tender breath stirs leaves above,
A soft caress, like whispered love.

Stars peek through the emerald cloak,
As the woods awaken, softly spoke.
Beneath their watch, the world transforms,
From silent peace to wild storms.

The rustle of wings, a fleeting sigh,
Awakens secrets in the night sky.
Under the arch of the ancient oaks,
Nature hums her timeless jokes.

Each glade echoes tales of old,
Of dreams forgotten and stories bold.
Among the boughs, mysteries creep,
As nightfall whispers, the forest keeps.

In this dark realm, enchantments weave,
Where lingering shadows never leave.
So close your eyes and let it be,
Nightfall's breath will set you free.

Echoes of Color and Change

Beneath the boughs where colors clash,
Leaves shimmer bright in a vibrant splash.
Autumn's breath, a painter's hand,
Transforming life across the land.

The golden hues in daylight fade,
As twilight whispers the night's parade.
Crimson flames dance on branches bare,
Each gust of wind a lively flare.

Fading greens from summer's throne,
Glow in the dusk, yet feel alone.
For every season must take its turn,
In the dance of life, we twist and learn.

Frost will crack the boldest dye,
Yet in their quiet, we learn to fly.
Through echoes of change, we find our place,
In the cycle of time, we embrace grace.

So live with color, shine your light,
For beauty lingers in the night.
In ebb and flow, let your heart range,
In the whispers of life, we're ever strange.

Laughter of Leaves in the Breeze

In the gentle sway of trees,
Where whispers dance on summer's breeze,
Green laughter flits from bough to bough,
A secret song known only now.

Sunlight filters through the shade,
Each glimmering spot a playful aid,
While shadows play their games of hide,
In nature's arms, where dreams abide.

The rustling leaves, a joyful sound,
Entwine the heart, and joy is found,
As breezes carry tales untold,
Of every wonder, young and old.

The woodland glows with life and cheer,
In every twist, a little tear,
Of happiness that fills the air,
In laughter shared, a bond that's rare.

So wander here, where leaves do laugh,
Find solace in this verdant path,
For in the rustle, love appears,
A symphony that soothes our fears.

The Forgotten Tales of the Forest

In shadows deep where stories sleep,
Amid the pines, old secrets keep,
With every rustle, time awakes,
To share the fables that the forest makes.

Once chanted songs of ancient trees,
Still linger lightly with the breeze,
Each gnarled root, a page of lore,
Whispers of magic forevermore.

The owls, they gaze with knowing eyes,
Relaying truths in moonlit skies,
Their hoots compose an echoing tale,
Of love and loss that will not pale.

The forest floor, a tapestry,
Of memories, daunting as the sea,
With every step on fallen leaf,
We gather stories, joy, and grief.

So pause and listen, hear them call,
The tales of time that beckon all,
For in the forest's silence, bright,
Lie echoes of forgotten light.

Hidden Realms in the Golden Mist

Through silver fog and golden light,
Where dreams can dance in soft twilight,
The hidden realms invite the bold,
To seek the wonders yet untold.

With every step, the mists enfold,
A world where secrets do not grow old,
Where laughter sparkles on the stream,
And every shadow hides a dream.

Across the glades, the fairies flit,
With stories woven, bit by bit,
In twilight's grasp, they twirl and play,
As dusk and dawn entwine their sway.

Here time does waver, breathe, and sigh,
As fleeting moments weave and fly,
Their magic lingers in the glow,
Of realms where only dreamers go.

So wander softly, heart aglow,
In golden mist, let spirits flow,
For hidden realms await your gaze,
With promises of endless days.

Journey Through the Last Light

As twilight falls on weary trails,
The last light dances, gently pales,
With every footstep, shadows creep,
And hold the echoes of our deep.

The fading sun, a painter's brush,
Strokes of gold in a softened hush,
Guiding hearts through night's embrace,
Where dreams and reality interlace.

A path unfurls, the stars align,
In whispered secrets, they entwine,
Each heartbeat echoes in the vast,
A journey forward, never past.

Through darkened woods, the courage grows,
With every twist that fate bestows,
For in the journey, light will find,
The strength to shatter night's unkind.

So follow where the last light leads,
Through mysteries of heart and seeds,
For in the quiet, hope ignites,
And dreams alight in starry nights.

Tales of the Grove in Transition

In the heart of the grove, secrets lie,
Branches sway gently, under the sky.
Whispers of change in the soft evening light,
Nature's embrace wraps the world in delight.

Leaves fall like dreams, swirling in air,
A tapestry woven, with love and with care.
Each rustle a story, each shadow a muse,
In this sacred sanctuary, we wander and choose.

Beneath the old oak, memories gleam,
Echoes of laughter flow like a stream.
Roots intertwine, holding time in their grasp,
As we seek the magic, in each moment we clasp.

The wildflowers bloom, painting the ground,
A dance of colors, where peace can be found.
In the twilight's hush, even starlight concedes,
That every transition is born from new seeds.

So heed the grove's tales, as seasons reform,
Embrace the unknown, let your spirit be warm.
For change is a journey, alight with new grace,
And the grove holds the answers, in time's gentle pace.

Serene Murmurs from the Leafy Depths

In the leafy depths, a whisper flows,
Murmurs of calm, where the soft wind blows.
Cascading shadows dance on the ground,
In this tranquil haven, peace can be found.

Beneath the branches, stories unfold,
Of ancient secrets and treasures untold.
A chorus of rustling, a symphony near,
Nature's sweet lullaby, soothing and clear.

The dappled sunlight weaves through the trees,
Carrying tales on the gentle breeze.
Each fluttering leaf holds a note of the past,
In this place of wonder, the echoes will last.

With every step on the mossy trail,
The heart beats softly, a delicate tale.
The harmony whispers through roots in the earth,
In this sacred stillness, we find our rebirth.

As dusk paints the world in shades of deep blue,
The murmurs grow louder, each moment feels new.
In the leafy depths, we find our embrace,
Serene, we linger, in nature's warm grace.

The Owls' Serenade at Sundown

As the sun dips low, the owls take flight,
In the hush of dusk, we welcome the night.
With feathers of velvet and eyes like the stars,
They sing to the shadows of ancient memoirs.

Perched high on a branch, they hoot their refrain,
A melody woven through twilight's soft grain.
Each note tells a story of wisdom and care,
Of secrets unfolding in cool evening air.

In the stillness, their voices blend tight,
A serenade echoing through the dark night.
As the moon rises high, a silver embrace,
We listen, enchanted, in this hallowed space.

The forest becomes a stage of delight,
Where echoes of laughter fade into night.
With owls as our guide, and shadows as friends,
The serenade lingers; our spirits transcends.

So when dusk descends and the world turns to rest,
Find solace in sounds that the night has expressed.
The owls remind us, as they sing their sweet song,
That magic is woven where we all belong.

Breezes Carrying Stories Long Forgotten

Through the ancient trees, a whisper drifts,
Breezes that carry the world's lost gifts.
Echoes of laughter, of joy and of pain,
Stories forgotten, called back once again.

As the light fades softly, shadows entwine,
The secrets of ages, in moonlight they shine.
Each gust of the wind holds a tale of the past,
In the dance of the leaves, with the die ever cast.

Gentle reminders of moments long gone,
In the heart of the grove, they linger on.
With every soft sigh, the stories arise,
Carried on breezes, beneath starlit skies.

The fragrance of memories drifts like a dream,
Weaving around us, a delicate seam.
In the quiet embrace of the night's gentle breath,
The lore of the ancients speaks even in death.

So listen intently, to whispers so sweet,
The breezes hold tales of heartbeats discreet.
For in every rustle, a fragment remains,
A journey of spirits that time never drains.

The Gentle Fall of Nature's Gold

Leaves tumble softly, a whispering sigh,
A dance of old gold beneath the grey sky.
The earth wears a blanket, so rich and so bright,
As nature retreats into the cool of the night.

The branches extend, like arms to the air,
Holding the secrets they choose to not share.
Each flutter, a story, each rustle, a glance,
Of moments enchanted in a quiet dance.

The chill of the twilight, a moment to pause,
As shadows grow longer, they bask in applause.
The whispers of autumn, a tender refrain,
Invite the lost summer to dance once again.

In puddles reflecting the light of the moon,
You hear nature's heartbeat, a gentle tune.
The colors cascade, in a glorious fight,
As day surrenders to the soft arms of night.

With each fallen leaf, comes a tale to be spun,
Of laughter and longing, of sorrow and fun.
The gentle fall beckons, a time to behold,
In the hush of the forest, where stories unfold.

Mysteries Beneath the Canopy

Beneath the green quilt, ancient secrets lie,
Whispers of creatures that flit and that fly.
Moss-covered stones, like faded old prints,
Hide tales of the forest, in shadows they glint.

Roots intertwine, like fingers in trust,
Holding the stories of life in the dust.
The silence is heavy, yet full of delight,
As wishes take flight within the still night.

A glimmer of eyes, in the dark they appear,
Watchful and wise, full of myth and of fear.
The heartbeat of nature echoes so deep,
In secrets that linger where shadows creep.

Phosphorescent fungi in silence glow bright,
Illuminating paths through the magical night.
Each footstep a journey, each breath, a soft song,
Inviting the lost ones to dance along.

So tread with respect, in this wonder-filled place,
For mysteries linger in each hidden space.
The canopy whispers, the night will unfold,
Revealing the wonders beneath, yet untold.

Silhouettes of the Enchanted Grove

In twilight's embrace, trees stand tall and proud,
Their silhouettes dance, cloaked in a shroud.
Each branch a soft whisper, each leaf a great sigh,
As day fades away, and stars start to rise.

The moon bathes the grove in a silvery hue,
While shadows play games, weaving old with the new.
Creatures of dusk stir, beginning their quest,
In the heart of the glen, where magic finds rest.

A breeze weaves through boughs, a sweet lullaby,
Reminding the earth of the days passing by.
A tapestry vast, stitched with heart's gentle thread,
Where every soft sigh invites dreams to be fed.

Glimmers of fireflies trace patterns in flight,
Their glow like the stars, twinkling in the night.
The air fills with stories of ages gone past,
In shadows unbroken, where memories last.

Lost voices of faeries, in whispers they call,
In the stillness of night, they invite one and all.
As silence envelops, and dreams start to weave,
In the enchanted grove, where hearts truly believe.

Rustling Tales of the Woodland

In the heart of the wood, where the wild creatures roam,
Tales rustle like leaves, inviting us home.
The brook softly bubbling, a melody sweet,
Carries the stories of all that we meet.

The owl calls at dusk, a wise elder's hymn,
While shadows stretch long and the light starts to dim.
Every crack of a twig stirs the spirits awake,
Telling of magic, of love, and heartache.

The fox with its cunning, darts here and then there,
Weaving through underbrush, with elegance rare.
Nature's own playwright, scripting life with such grace,
In the forest's soft clutches, there's a warm embrace.

The trees lean in close, like old friends at a feast,
Sharing their whispers, their thoughts unleashed.
With every rustling leaf, a story unfurls,
Of battles and triumphs, of boys and of girls.

The night deepens softly, as stars wink above,
The woodland is woven with secrets of love.
So gather your courage, let your heart be a friend,
In rustling tales sung, where beginnings won't end.

The Elven Path in Rustling Silence

In twilight's grasp the shadows creep,
Where ancient whispers softly weep.
A winding trail of silver light,
Leads us through the fading night.

Beneath the boughs of emerald leaf,
Time holds its breath, a moment brief.
With every step, the silence sings,
Of secrets known to woodland things.

The air is thick with magic's breath,
As nature dances, defying death.
A glimmer here, a flicker there,
Elven laughter fills the air.

In hidden glades where wild things play,
The heart finds solace, lost in sway.
With every rustle, hope ignites,
In the embrace of starry nights.

So tread with care on paths unseen,
Where dreams unfold and hearts convene.
For through the quiet, life will bloom,
And every step dispels the gloom.

Gilded Memories Underfoot

Beneath our feet, the leaves do crunch,
A symphony of autumn's lunch.
Each golden hue a tale to tell,
Of fleeting moments, where we dwell.

In sunlit hours, we wander free,
Through fields of gold, by ancient trees.
The past is woven in each stride,
With memories forever tied.

The laughter echoes in the breeze,
Like whispers caught among the trees.
We gather dreams as shadows fall,
Both grand and small, we cherish all.

Each step a breadcrumb in the years,
A map of joy, a weave of fears.
Yet still, they guide us on our way,
To brighter skies and hope's array.

So as we tread on gilded ground,
Let love and laughter be the sound.
For with each memory we ignite,
We paint our lives in colors bright.

Secrets Woven in Nature's Quilt

In tangled roots, our secrets lie,
Beneath the arch of shaded sky.
With whispered winds that weave their tales,
Through glades where sunlight never pales.

The brook's soft murmur tells a story,
Of hidden paths and fleeting glory.
In every rustle, every call,
Nature's secrets hold us all.

The flowers bloom with vibrant grace,
In colors soft, a warm embrace.
Each petal speaks of worlds unseen,
Of bonds that linger, evergreen.

Among the trees, wisdom resides,
In silent grace, where magic hides.
With every look, a spell is cast,
In nature's quilt, the present and past.

So listen close, and you may find,
The gifts of earth, so gently lined.
For in the quiet, secrets soar,
Embedding life forevermore.

Luminous Twilight Over Whispering Thickets

The twilight gleams, a soft embrace,
As shadows dance in twilight's space.
Amidst the thickets, secrets swell,
In whispered tones, the night will tell.

A glow ignites the world around,
With silver rays on hallowed ground.
In every heart, the dreams ignite,
Preparing souls for coming night.

In twilight's hush, the creatures stir,
With gentle wings, a quiet blur.
The stars awaken, one by one,
As day departs, and night's begun.

With bated breath, we stand in awe,
Of nature's magic, pure and raw.
The darkness hums a lullaby,
Inviting hearts to softly sigh.

So let us wander, hand in hand,
Through whispering thickets, o'er golden sand.
For in this hour of fading light,
Our spirits soar, forever bright.

Celestial Dance of Twilight Spirits

In twilight's grasp, the spirits twirl,
A dance of shadows, swift and swirl.
Beneath the moon's soft silver grace,
They weave their tales in a timeless space.

With whispers sweet, the night unfolds,
Each secret glimmeringly holds.
As stars ignite in velvet skies,
The world awakes through ancient cries.

A chorus echoes through the vale,
As dreams and wishes set their sail.
In harmony, they glide and spin,
Inviting hearts to drift within.

The fireflies flicker in delight,
While shadows play in pale moonlight.
A tapestry of endless night,
Where spirits dance, and souls take flight.

So join the revel, let time unwind,
In twilight's embrace, together aligned.
For in this realm where magic thrives,
The celestial dance forever lives.

Traces of Time on the Forest Path

Upon the path where silence sighs,
Footprints linger, as time flies.
The trees stand tall, with tales to share,
Each rustling leaf a whispered prayer.

Moss blankets stones, both old and wise,
Each crack and crevice holds the skies.
Beneath the boughs where shadows play,
The memories linger and softly sway.

Beneath the arches, the sunlight beams,
Guiding wanderers through their dreams.
A tapestry of green and gold,
In every twist, a story told.

Echoes of laughter float like mist,
Wrapped in nature's gentle tryst.
Each bend reveals a hidden glade,
Where time stands still and moments wade.

So tread with grace on this sacred ground,
In every heartbeat, magic's found.
For on this path, where shadows dwell,
The traces of time weave their spell.

Harvest Moon Over Enchanted Roots

The harvest moon, so bright and round,
Casts its glow on the fertile ground.
With fields aglow in amber light,
The world awakens to magic's height.

Beneath its gaze, the roots entwine,
In whispered dreams, the vines define.
Fruits of labor, kissed by dew,
A bounty rich, in colors true.

As lanterns flicker in the breeze,
The earth hums softly with ancient pleas.
With every step, the magic flows,
In gratitude, the harvest grows.

The essence of joy fills the night air,
With laughter echoing everywhere.
Dancing shadows, a joyous spree,
United under the moonlit sea.

So gather round, let hearts unite,
In celebration of love's pure light.
For when the harvest moon appears,
Enchanted roots shall banish fears.

The Breath of the Wind in the Thicket

In thickets dense, the whispers roam,
Carried by wind that calls us home.
Through tangled branches, secrets weave,
A heart's adventure, believe, believe.

The breath of wind sings sweet refrains,
Soft melodies, like gentle rains.
It lifts the spirit, sets it free,
In every gust, a mystery.

Leaves flutter down, a graceful dance,
While shadows twirl in nature's trance.
Each echo tells a tale of old,
In every breeze, a dream unfolds.

The thicket shimmers with life anew,
As nature's breath makes spirits stew.
Embracing all the wild and free,
In this sanctuary, we long to be.

So let the wind guide you along,
In its embrace, you'll find your song.
For in the thicket, life's true gift,
Is the breath of the wind, a timeless lift.

Fables of the Fallen Boughs

In twilight whispers tales unfold,
Of branches bowed and stories told.
The moonlight weaves through shadows near,
While ancient spirits dance with cheer.

The winds carry secrets through the night,
Of dreams once lost, now taking flight.
Beneath the starlit canopy's grace,
The echoes linger in this sacred space.

Each leaf that drifts tells of the past,
Of moments cherished, love that lasts.
The earth below, a soft embrace,
Holds all the magic of this place.

In silence, wisdom softly grows,
As time weaves tales the heart knows.
For in each bough that bends and sways,
Lies the truth of fables sung in praise.

So gather 'round, let spirits soar,
In fallen boughs, we find much more.
With every breath, a legend speaks,
Of lives entwined, the past it seeks.

Carved in the Essence of Decay

Amidst the crumbling stones we find,
The beauty wrapped in nature's bind.
Decay reveals the soul's true art,
A canvas painted from the heart.

Each withering petal, each rusted gate,
Speaks of the passage, the hands of fate.
The colors fade, yet softly glow,
In every crack, a story flows.

Moss blankets walls like emerald lace,
Whispers of time in this sacred space.
The essence of life, in shadows cast,
Reminds us of moments that never last.

For life and death dance hand in hand,
In every ruin, in every strand.
From ashes rise the seeds of dreams,
In decay's embrace, all is not as it seems.

So celebrate what once held sway,
In the silent art of decay.
For beauty lies where few may dare,
In forgotten places, a story rare.

The Echo of Wings Among the Trees

High above, the shadows gleam,
Where whispers dwell and wild hearts dream.
The flutter of wings, a soft refrain,
Calls forth the magic in the rain.

Through branches thick and twilight's mist,
A tapestry of hope persists.
The owls watch over, wise and bright,
Guardians of secrets hidden from sight.

Each rustle brings a gentle sigh,
Of stories woven in the sky.
The fluttering leaves, a quiet choir,
Sing of wishes, of hearts on fire.

With every beat, the echoes soar,
Reminders of dreams forever more.
In twilight's glow, the shadows play,
As wings declare the end of day.

So let your spirit rise and fly,
Among the trees and starry sky.
For in the echo of wings that soar,
Lies the magic we all adore.

Rituals of the Woodland Realm

In hidden glades where silence reigns,
The woodland sings of ancient planes.
Rituals echo in the dappled light,
Awakening dreams in the hush of night.

Gather 'round, the fire ignites,
With whispered words and sacred rites.
Nature's chorus joins the throng,
In unity, we find our song.

The stones align, with purpose grand,
As we invoke the spirits' hand.
In every flicker, an ember glows,
Of love and loss, as the river flows.

In this realm, where shadows weave,
The heart of magic, we believe.
For every tree and every stone,
Holds the essence of what is grown.

So let us dance in moonlit streams,
And weave our hopes in sacred dreams.
In the woodland's embrace, we find,
A tapestry of the intertwined.

The Voice of the Woodland Spirits

In the heart of the woods so deep,
Where whispers of magic softly creep,
The spirits sing with a gentle grace,
Their voices dance in a timeless space.

Under the boughs, the secrets hide,
A tapestry woven where shadows bide,
With every breeze, their stories flow,
In echoes where the wildflowers grow.

They beckon the lost with a soothing tune,
Beneath the glow of a silver moon,
In every rustle, there's wisdom shared,
A magic world that has always cared.

Leaves flutter softly, a soft refrain,
Riding the currents of joy and pain,
Through ancient oaks, their laughter rings,
Awakening dreams on enchanted wings.

So if you wander, keep your heart free,
For the woodland spirits weave harmony,
In the space between earth and sky,
Their whispers linger, forever nigh.

Faded Legends Beneath Our Feet

Beneath the soil, where stories lie,
Of ancient heroes who dared to fly,
Faded legends in the earth confined,
Whispers of battles within the mind.

Each stone a tale, each root a rhyme,
Echoing softly through the threads of time,
Guardians of dreams, the earth entwines,
With secrets buried in twisted vines.

The grass sways gently, a cloak of green,
Covering stories we've never seen,
Yet when we listen, the past reveals,
A world of wonder in delicate seals.

With every step on soft, muted ground,
The echoes of lives once lost resound,
A patchwork of histories interlace,
Faded whispers from a forgotten place.

Take heed of the ground beneath your tread,
For faded legends have not truly fled,
Each breath we take, each moment spent,
Binds us to stories that never relent.

Fragments of a Fading Day

As the sun dips low, the shadows blend,
A canvas painted as day must end,
Fragments of light in a golden hue,
Whispering secrets of dreams come true.

The skies ablaze with the twilight's fire,
Glimmers of hope in a world that's dire,
Each ray a promise, a fleeting sigh,
Bidding farewell to the day gone by.

Stars awaken, their twinkle soft,
As night descends, the world drifts aloft,
In the fading twilight, soft shadows play,
Carrying whispers of the fading day.

Moonlight dances on the silver streams,
Courting the echoes of long-lost dreams,
Each moment lingers in twilight's fold,
Weaving stories in hues of gold.

So hold tight the fragments, for they are rare,
The beauty of dusk lingers in the air,
In the silence that follows, find your way,
Embrace the magic of the fading day.

A Journey Through Rustic Hues

In a world where colors softly blend,
A journey awaits around every bend,
Through rustic hues of emerald green,
And fields of gold, a tranquil scene.

Footpaths winding beneath the trees,
Whispers of history ride on the breeze,
Every leaf tells a tale untold,
Of laughter, of love, in shades of gold.

Crimson sunsets that kiss the land,
Painting the valleys with a loving hand,
The sky ablaze, a vibrant view,
Each stroke a story, each moment new.

Amidst the quiet, a song will rise,
In hues of twilight, a sweet surprise,
Nature sings with an ageless sound,
Inviting us to tread the sacred ground.

So join the journey through rustic hues,
Let the colors inspire your muse,
In every shade, a world unfolds,
A tapestry rich with stories told.

Starlit Paths Through the Glade

In the hush of night so deep,
Whispers in the shadows creep,
Paths of silver, softly gleam,
Guiding souls towards a dream.

Trees adorned with glowing lights,
Dancing in the gentle nights,
Footfalls light as whispered sighs,
Underneath the vast, wide skies.

Moonbeams weave a tapestry,
Waking hearts with mystery,
Every step a spell so bright,
Leading onward, pure delight.

In the glade, where secrets rest,
Nature's magic is the best,
With each breath, enchantments swell,
Starlit paths weave tales to tell.

Autumn's Lament Across the Clearing

Leaves descend with softest grace,
Painting earth with nature's lace,
Whispers echo in the breeze,
Autumn's sigh 'midst golden trees.

Echoes of the summer's cheer,
Fading fast as winter's near,
A tapestry of red and gold,
A story of the leaves retold.

Crisp air brings a wistful tune,
Beneath the watch of waning moon,
Every rustle tells a tale,
Of seasons past and dreams that sail.

In the clearing, shadows long,
Nature's chorus, sweet and strong,
As branches sway, the memories cling,
In autumn's grasp, the songbirds sing.

The Color of Forgotten Dreams

In the quiet of the night,
Colors fade and lose their light,
Whispers of what once had been,
Echo through the spaces green.

Lost in realms where shadows play,
Where the heart's desires stray,
Hues of longing paint the air,
Shimmering with unspoken care.

Dreams like petals, soft and frail,
Drift like ships upon a sail,
Each one holds a story dear,
Colors bright yet veiled in fear.

In the tapestry of night,
Forgotten dreams take wing to flight,
As the dawn begins to gleam,
We remember what we dream.

Petals on the Breath of Twilight

In twilight's hush, the petals fall,
Painting whispers, soft and small,
Carried on the evening air,
Gentle sighs, a fragrant fair.

Colors blend, a soft embrace,
Lacing dusk with tender grace,
Every bloom, a sweet farewell,
Casts a spell, the heart can tell.

As shadows stretch and mingle near,
Petals scatter, rise and clear,
On the breath of night, they sway,
Guiding dreams that softly play.

In the stillness, stories weave,
Echoes linger, hearts believe,
Petals dancing in the light,
On the breath of endless night.

Wandering Through Shimmering Shadows

In twilight's embrace where whispers reside,
I wander 'neath the stars that confide.
The shadows dance with a silvery gleam,
As I drift through the night, lost in a dream.

Trees murmur secrets, their branches entwined,
Each rustle a story, by moonlight designed.
The path is a ribbon of mystery spun,
Leading me deeper till day is undone.

A chime in the darkness, a flicker of light,
Guides me through shadows, soft, gentle, bright.
With every step deeper, the world feels more real,
In shimmering echoes my heart learns to feel.

The night air is rich with a magical touch,
As stars weave their tales in the silence, so much.
I linger, enchanted, as dreams intertwine,
In this realm of shadows where realities align.

With dawn on the horizon, my journey must cease,
But the shimmering shadows grant me sweet peace.
I'll carry their whispers, forever I'll roam,
In the heart of the night, I've found my true home.

A Tapestry of Nature's Farewell

In autumn's embrace, the leaves start to fall,
A tapestry woven, a clear siren call.
Golden and crimson, they swish in the breeze,
Painting the ground like a soft, whispered tease.

The trees bow in sorrow, their branches laid bare,
As nature prepares for a long, tender care.
Each cackle of crows adds a note to the song,
In this symphony vibrant, where seasons belong.

The river, once lively, now murmurs a tune,
Reflecting the colors of harvest and moon.
In the hush of the evening, I breathe in the air,
Filled with the essence of love, wild and rare.

A gust carries whispers of chill and of change,
As clouds weave their blankets, vast and strange.
The farewell of nature is bittersweet grace,
In the dance of the seasons, we find our place.

So gather your treasures, the memories near,
For though nature weeps, it will soon reappear.
In cycles unending, life's beauty prevails,
A tapestry spun with the softest of trails.

Mosaics of Wood and Time

In forests enchanted, where whispers unite,
A mosaic of wood tells of day and of night.
Knots tell of journeys, of storms and of calm,
Each ring a reminder, a timeless old psalm.

I wander through groves, where history breathes,
With each step I sift through the leaves and the seeds.
The roots twist like dreams, grounded yet free,
In a carpet of stories, a spell over me.

Branches stretch skyward, a quest for the light,
In each leaf's fragile grip the stars take flight.
Memories linger, like dew on the dawn,
In the heart of the forest, I feel I belong.

From the hush of the pine to the oak's sturdy might,
Each tree tells a tale in the softening light.
The echoes of ages resonate clear,
A song of the ancients, rich and sincere.

So let me be cradled in nature's embrace,
For in her great wisdom, I find my own place.
In mosaics of wood, in the weave of the time,
I discover my spirit, my essence, my rhyme.

Leaping Sparks of Autumn's Fire

In twilight's embrace, the bonfire ignites,
Leaping sparks dance wildly, like stars in their flights.
The crackle and pop weave their tales in the night,
As flames twist and twirl, a flickering light.

Golden leaves gather, a carpet so bright,
Whispers of autumn accompany night.
The laughter of friends fills the cool, crisp air,
As stories unfold, with moments to share.

Each ember a wish, rising high to the sky,
In this warmth of togetherness, spirits fly.
With flavors of spices and cider, we cheer,
Embraced by the glow, surrounded by dear.

The harvest moon watches, a sentinel bright,
As shadows grow long, signifying delight.
In the magic of autumn, our hearts intertwine,
With leaping sparks singing, in rhythms divine.

So gather your dreams as we bid day adieu,
In this hypnotic dance, life begins anew.
As embers extinguish, we'll carry the flame,
For each spark ignited is never the same.

The Last Flicker of Autumn's Glow

As leaves descend in swirling flight,
The whispering winds draw close at night.
A world once ablaze with golden cheer,
Now cradles the chill of a coming year.

Beneath the boughs, a silent tale,
Of fleeting warmth as shadows pale.
Each crackling step on frosted ground,
Holds echoes of summer, softly drowned.

The sunset bleeds in hues so bright,
A final blush before the night.
Nature pauses, in quiet awe,
Embracing the stillness, its solemn law.

Yet cheer remains in the fading light,
With fireflies dancing, a splendid sight.
For every end, a new dawn waits,
In cycles of life, our heart celebrates.

So gather 'round, as dusk descends,
For autumn's glow, the heart defends.
In memory bright, the warmth we know,
Lingers ever in the last flicker's glow.

Secrets of the Sylvan Realm

In twilight's hush, the trees confide,
Whispering secrets, ancient, wide.
A world of magic, hidden deep,
Where sylvan spirits laugh and leap.

Among the ferns, the shadows play,
Creation's brush in twilight's sway.
With every breeze, a tale unfolds,
Of fae and dreams, and starlit golds.

The brook sings soft in crystal tones,
Guarding the echoes of crumbled stones.
Each ripple a memory of long ago,
In the heart of woods where wonders grow.

Moss-clad stones in a verdant maze,
Guide the lost through evening's haze.
In the grove's heart, a light so rare,
Time freezes still — the sylvan air.

So listen close; the trees invite,
To share in secrets veiled from sight.
In every whisper, magic swells,
In the sylvan realm where silence dwells.

A Gracious Ending in Soft Hues

The sun dips low in a velvet sky,
Casting shadows where soft whispers lie.
A final bow, the day takes flight,
Drifting gently into the night.

Clouds kiss the horizon, blushing pink,
As stars awaken, letting thoughts sink.
Each heartbeat echoes in harmony,
A gracious ending, soft as can be.

Bathed in gold, the world stands still,
With every sunset, time does fill.
Nature's palette, a masterpiece drawn,
Fleeting moments, forever gone.

The moon arises, a watchful eye,
Guiding dreams like clouds drifting high.
With tender strokes of silence anew,
A graceful farewell in the evening's hue.

So let us linger where shadows play,
In the fading light of the closing day.
For in each ending, beauty takes flight,
In the soft embrace of a velvet night.

Feathered Friends of the Twilight Glade

In twilight's grasp, the woodlands sing,
With melodies woven on flapping wing.
Feathered friends in colors so bright,
Dance 'neath the stars, a dazzling sight.

The robin's call, a soothing sound,
Weaves through the trees, echoing round.
While sparrows flit, with cheerful glee,
In the arms of dusk, forever free.

The owl, so wise, perched high above,
Watches with patience, a guardian of love.
As night spreads slowly, a silken shroud,
The glade turns mystical, bathed in cloud.

Each chirp and coo a gentle sigh,
Nature's heartbeat in the velvety sky.
Fluttering wings in the softening light,
Cloak the glade in whispers of night.

So gather near, let the dusk enfold,
The secrets of twilight in stories told.
For in this haven, as dreams ignite,
Feathered friends bring magic to the night.

9 781805 635611